My Little Peanut Does the Nuttiest Things!

Humor & Rhymes

Normandy D. Piccolo
Elizabeth Marie A.

NBI
Normandy's Bright Ideas
Florida

"Children are unpredictable. You never know what inconsistency they're going to catch you in next."

~ Franklin P. Jones

INTRODUCTION

My little peanut does the nuttiest things
After a turn of the page you will see what I mean

I love my little peanut, as you love yours, too
But as a parent you can't help but wonder, why do kids do
what they do?

IS IT JUST MY IMAGINATION?

My little peanut is on a hot trend
Having conjured up a new imaginary friend
This invisible character is quite a loose end
And about to send this Mommy off to the looney bin

"Who colored my bedspread in black sharpie ink?"
"Tony did mommy!" my little peanut replied with a wink.
"Where is my expensive stole, the one that is mink?"
"Tony thought it was smelly. It's soaking in the kitchen sink."

Apparently, Tony is rather a crafty little scamp
Per my little peanut, he even broke my new lamp.
I cannot see Tony, the infamous destructive champ
For if I did, in the mail he would go, signed, sealed
and under a stamp.

NOODLE HEAD

My little peanut did not like his cut hair
He cried his eyes out while in the barber's chair
Once the haircut was over, he shot me a glare
Having changed from a toddler into an angry old bear

Oh, how he despised his very first hair cut
He pulled at the roots, a pouty lip he did jut
The entire ride home his mouth refused to stay shut
Screaming as if he had been socked in the gut

Later that night at around dinner time
He sat in the high chair silent as a mime
So, quiet in fact, it was almost sublime
Until he lifted-up his bowl and then it was show time

A bowl of spaghetti he spilled onto his head
The noodles draped down like soggy old bread
My face changed from normal to totally red
"Look mommy! I got my hair back", he happily said.

ARE WE THERE YET?

Off on a road trip our family goes
Seeing the United States from head to toe
Baby wipes, snacks, blankets and comfy clothes
Taking our time, not driving too fast, nor to slow

Ten minutes in and the little peanut screams out my name
"Mommy! Mommy! I want to play a game!"
"Alphabet, I Spy", I reply, "Those are fun games."
"No Mommy! No! Those games are all lame!"

So, I ask my little peanut, "What game shall we play?"
My little peanut smiles and then takes it away,
"Are we there yet? Are we there yet? Are we there yet?"
Like a donkey, for the next 100 miles he repeatedly braes.

The four-worded question every parent does dread
Like a broken tape recorder, it gets stuck inside your head
Over and over as it is asked again and again, "Are we there yet?
Are we there yet?" as you rub your aching forehead.

WHY? BECAUSE I SAID SO

When my little peanut spoke his very first word
I was filled with much joy, my emotions so stirred
It was the most adorable sound a parent ever heard
That first word he spoke, oh, my nutty little nerd

Now some days I wish my little peanut would not speak
I would even settle for an hour of a good tantrum shriek
No, I am not at all being tongue in cheek
For my little peanut, is on a one-word streak

WHY?

"Why?", he asks of me, "Why?"
"Because I said so", I firmly reply.
"Why?" he asks again, attempting to pry.
"Because I said so", I reply, before ending with a sigh

"Why?"
"Because I said so."
"Why?"
"Because. I. Said. So."

My little peanut's why's continue, no end in sight
Until the clock strikes seven and so begins the plight
The why's finally growing silent after the routine big fight
For the time has come for my little peanut to say "Goodnight."

I SHARED MY BAH-SKETTI

Nothing says mommy like that 2:00 AM wake-up call
Your little peanut towering over you, appearing ten feet tall
Half in a daze you ask, "Does your tummy hurt you?"
When food from your little peanut's mouth begins to spew

Yuck! Gag! Retch! I try not to puke, too
Grabbing my little peanut now painted in tonight's dinner goo
As I prepare to cover his mouth and make a dash for the loo
My little peanut cries out, "Look Mommy! I just shared my
bah-sketti with you!"

I want to reply with a resounding, "Ewwww!"
Staring down at my sick little peanut wondering what to do
But the mommy in me who longs to stay true
Instead smiles and utters a reply of "Aww, thank you."

DOODLES

My little peanut is an apparent doodle bug
With a paintbrush in hand, he runs and gives me a hug
As I glance over his shoulder, happiness fades from my mug
For he has connected the spots on our pet Dalmatian dog –
"Ugh!"

NO!

It was so cute when my little peanut first learned to speak
His lips formed funny shapes, his voice it did squeak
"Momma", he finally cried out, with a proud hearty shriek
I hugged him so tightly and planted kisses on his cheek

But soon a new word would dominate his speech
Worse than anything that an angry preacher might preach
Oh, this certain word is quite the little peach
A word so annoying, one wishes they could unteach

"Pick up your toys and then we can go."
His answer, the infamous, "No! No! No!"
"Perhaps some time-out for that little show."
Once more, the naughty word pours forth,

"No!"

"No!"

"No!"

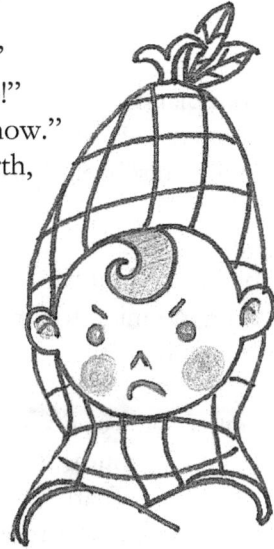

What does a parent do when a child refutes?
Aside from wanting to pull their own hair out by the roots
I mean, he's just a little peanut, not a big, bad brute
But oh, how he's transformed into quite the little snoot.

MY LITTLE FART

Musicians use instruments to create tunes of art
From pianos, to guitars, to harps they will start
A pot and a spoon first won my little peanut's heart
Until he discovered his own noisy fart

So, loud is his wind, it breaks the barrier of sound
My little peanut laughs as he falls to the ground
Paying no mind to who might be standing around
Ripping bean fueled tweets, he fancies himself quite profound

Toot! Toot! Toot!
My little peanut is in stitches
Toot! Toot! Tear!
He just tore a hole in his britches!

Choot! Choot! Choot!
Oh no! He has discovered a new hit
Choot! Choot! Choot!
As his hand gently, cups under his arm pit

The hilarity of passing gas my little peanut will not omit
Despite me often throwing a justified parental fit
Oh, how I wish this smelly habit he would soon quit
Even our poor pooch misses hearing, "The dog did it!"

NOSE PICKING

While one day at the store buying pantyhose
My little peanut began bugging me so -
I told him to look down and count his toes
But instead he did something peculiar with his nose

When I looked back my heart jumped into a flutter
My eyes bugged out, my body did shudder
For my little peanut's finger, had become a rudder
I hollered, "Stop pi-picking your no-nose!" in a frantic, stutter

My little peanut smiled and wondered I suppose
Thinking nothing wrong with having a finger up the nose
I giggled a bit, shook my head and then did mutter
As my little peanut offered me a glob of his peanut nose butter.

FAVORITE TOY

My little peanut has lost his favorite toy
He's wailing, gnashing and screaming, "Oi! Oi! Oi!"
Like any good Mommy I quickly develop a ploy
"I'll run to the store and buy him a decoy."

"I found it!" I cry upon sneaking back home from the store
My skeptical little peanut inspects the toy to the core
The next thing I know he drops it hard to the floor
Shouting "That's not my toy!" before slamming the door

I let out a sigh, knowing what must come next
This problem cannot be solved by writing a check
The time has come to stretch, flex and bend
And search the house for the toy, from end to end

I quietly scan his room with my trusty flashlight
When my eyes suddenly stop upon an unexpected sight
There cradled under his arms safe, warm and tight
My little peanut and his favorite toy -- they did reunite.

I WANNA WATCH IT AGAIN

Come TV-time and Mom and Dad want to retreat
To go hide inside a closet or rent a hotel suite
Why should they scatter and run in defeat?
Because of a cartoon being played on endless repeat

Over and over the same cartoon plays
Our little peanut giggles, staring, and locked in a haze
So many times, Mom and Dad are in a daze
What? The DVD player just broke! To the Lord we give praise!

STICKY JELLY FINGERS

My little peanut is by far the worst crook
Always trying to scam me with that innocent look
But the one thing that nails him each time on the hook
His grape jelly stained fingerprints speak like a babbling brook.

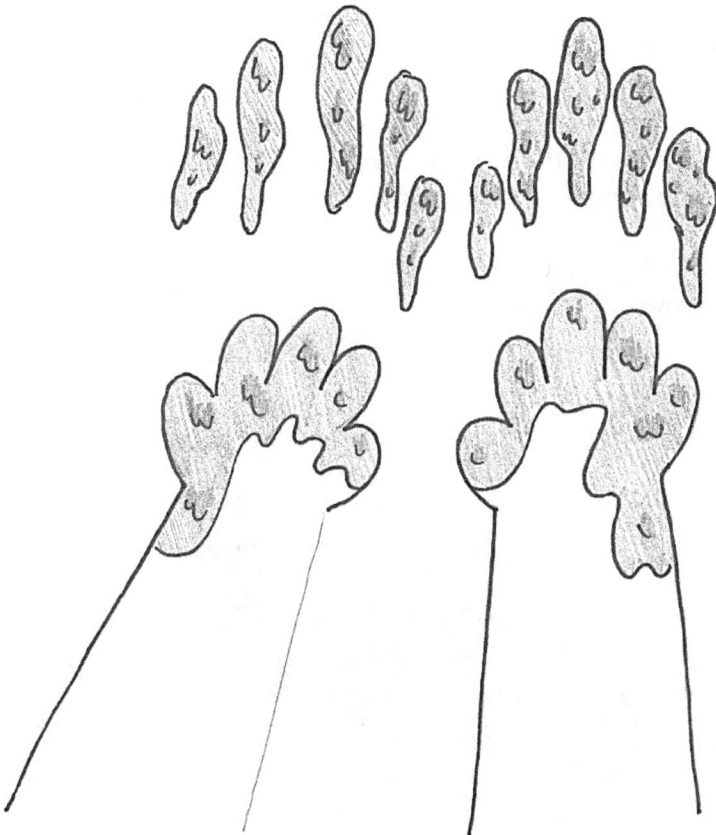

SELFIE KING

My little peanut did the sneakiest thing
And secretly knighted himself, a royal selfie-taking King
A hundred random photos of stuff he did bring
As my phone battery drained with each passing ping

When I went to use the cell phone, the battery was
mysteriously dead
"I charged it last night", I thought, "Am I losing my head?"
"I swore it had full bars", I stared down at it and said
"What could have happened? How could my eyes have
misread?"

Upon plugging in the charger, the answer soon was known
It was time for my little selfie-King to abdicate his throne
For Mommy, simply cannot function without a working cell
phone
When I calmly tried to explain this, peanut tantrums were
indeed thrown.

HOLY ROLIE POLIE

My little peanut is obsessed with bugs
Ants, crickets, worms, spiders and slugs
But one bug is receiving special types of hugs
And grossing mommy out, as she mutters repeated "Ughs!"

"Look, Mommy! Look!" he cries, shoving a roly poly in my face
And just like that I rocket from my kitchen into outer space
"Get that bug away from me!" I shout, rejecting his embrace
My little peanut cries, "But Mommy!" as he begins to give chase

Why do-little boys find roly polies to be so chummy?
Quite frankly they only churn this Mommy's delicate tummy
Then the unthinkable happened and my little peanut went glummy
He accidentally hugged the roly poly too tight between his finger and thumby.

HALO vs. HORNS

An angel in public, a devil at home
Around perfect strangers, wearing a crown made of chrome
But behind closed doors, he can be a vile, gnarly gnome
Perching those horns high up on his pointed fiendish dome

Smiling, cooing, giggling, in public he fools them all
An hour before, he had finger-painted the dining room wall
Next came duel tantrums, mine were big, his were small
Feeling completely exhausted, on the floor I did sprawl

Baby-talk, tickles and attention this kid will devour
But my sweet, charming little peanut will again turn sour
Once we are back home and it is bedtime hour
"Daddy come quickly! Mommy needs more manpower."

LICKITY SPLIT

Every kid adores their favorite treat
Whether a chocolate ice cream cone or a pickled beet
Some even like to nibble on their feet
While others snub vegetables, and only chew meat

My little peanut is rather unique
Some might even classify him as a freak
I'm not being at all tongue in cheek
For he has mastered himself quite an unusual technique

My nutty kid has developed the gall
He absolutely loves to lick every wall
Bathrooms, bedrooms and even the hall
Not to mention the dressing room stall at the mall

Wonder how long this peculiar phase will last
My throat is very sore from constant lambast
While kids will be kids, per the forecast
Can't wait 'til this whack-a-do stage is past.

NAPS

A mother's intuition knows when her little peanut needs a nap
Once whining and blubbering are all his lips dare flap
"It's naptime!" and he leaps right off her lap
Immediately growling like an angry bear caught in a trap

Begging with tears, the parent, not the child, will surely weep
In the vain hope of getting the little tyke to go to sleep
Back and forth protests and frustrations grow steep
Springing forth unkind mutters of "Just go to sleep you little
bleep!"

An hour of this routine is like doing a Pilates workout
Amazing how a kid can turn from candy into sauerkraut
What is it about taking a nap that causes a stomp and shout?
Either way, mommy needs a nap too, for she is officially wiped
out.

BUT I DON'T LIKE BROCCOLI!

Sooner or later every parent has this feud
The one when their kid denies a certain food
Their lips shut tight, arms crossed and acting rude
Leaving you feeling frustrated, baffled and completely skewed

I'll give you one guess who the contender is in the fight
Sometimes I think my little peanut refuses to eat it out of spite
Even with threats of no games and an early bedtime tonight
He declares himself the winner having not taken one broccoli bite.

LEGO DANCE

One wrong barefooted step and you do an aching prance
While your little peanut points at you in a giggling trance
Any parent of a toddler knows this doesn't happen perchance
It's the infamous 'I just stepped on a $%^& Lego' dance

You're suddenly thrust aboard the obscenity train
Foul words sprinkle forth from your mouth like pouring rain
You slap your hand over your trap, trying to control your brain
But alas, it can't be helped for the pain, oh, the pain!

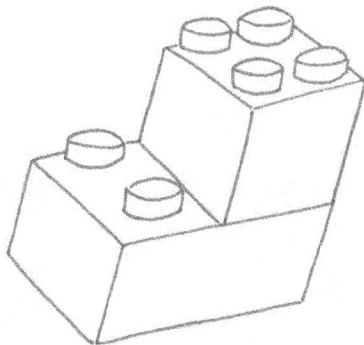

GOING COMMANDO

My little peanut often likes to go commando
Yanking off his clothes, sometimes in front of the window
Before dashing about the house like a crazy wild minnow
With clothes in hand, I try and put his streaking show in limbo

I had just got him dressed, his hair I did gel
Only to turn around and gasp, "What! Pray tell?"
Followed by the infamous "Go put on your shell!"
He just stared, shrugged his shoulders and said, "Oh well."

I immediately give chase, in my hand, a clean nappy
As he runs about the house feeling fresh and rather zappy
This mom is now bewildered, knackered and unhappy
Daring to bare it all, that's mommy's cheeky little chappy.

THE DAILY POOP

I have a self-proclaimed reporter who loves to share the scoop
Unfortunately, my little peanut's stories revolve around poop
The cat, the fish, the dog, the hamster, even the chicken coop
He'll share a story at dinnertime keeping his family in the loop.

DON'T ASK THAT

My little peanut caused my legs to turn to jelly
When he sauntered up to the counter one day at the deli
And unexpectedly asked a lady who was ordering vermicelli
"Is there a baby stuck inside your big ol' belly?"

Insulted the lady quickly snapped out a hearty, "No!"
"I am so sorry." I replied with my kid by the arm, in tow
"You shouldn't say things like to Mrs. So & So".
He looked up at me and innocently said, "Well, I didn't know."

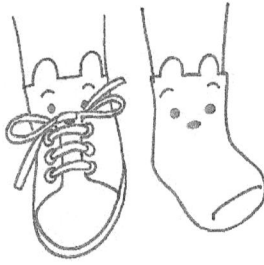

WHERE IS YOUR OTHER SHOE?

A big fight ensued while in route to the store
My little peanut cried out, "Shoe shopping is a bore!"
"Behave yourself and ice cream you will get," I pinky swore
He promised to do as I asked and not act rotten to the core

Two minutes in, he whined about using the loo
Five minutes in, a temper tantrum he up and threw
Fifteen minutes in, he had turned the store into a zoo
One hour later, we finally found the perfect shoe

He happily sat in the stroller as I gently pushed him along
Both of us giggling and chanting a silly cartoon song
Swinging his feet wildly about, not doing anything wrong
When he suddenly grew silent and his face appeared long

Glancing down I spied only a sock of Winnie the Pooh
I regretfully asked of him, "Where is your other new shoe?"
My little peanut shrugged his shoulders, not having a clue
The shoe forever lost, back to the store, for round two.

SLEEPY TIME

My little peanut enjoys napping in strange places
I'm fascinated by how he can fit into such tight spaces
Once I found him snuggled inside his daddy's open briefcase
He also squeezed himself between books inside the bookcase

Asleep in his cereal bowl while sitting in a highchair
Snoring while on the loo or with his tushy stuck up in the air
How he sleeps in such odd places, I wish he would share
As I write this, he has fallen asleep, this time on the stairs.

I WANT THE BOX

Christmas time and I became a stellar errand boy
Knowing my little peanut longed for the latest toy
Shopping during the holidays, one does not enjoy
But it is unavoidable, so one must plot, plan and ploy

I proudly placed the present under the tree like a fox
But Christmas morning, I needed some eggnog shots
For my kid was behaving rather odd and quite unorthodox
Instead of the toy, this kid was fascinated by the package box

From store to store I had traveled all day by train
Only to be told, 'We're sold out, but you can try again'.
But because I wouldn't' quit, the toy I did finally gain
Despite having developed the worst shopping migraine.

There's simply no use in becoming irate
He's ignoring the toy and instead playing with its crate
"Next holiday," I say, "Christmas shopping I shall negate"
Oh, who am I kidding. A new toy he wants, in line I shall wait.

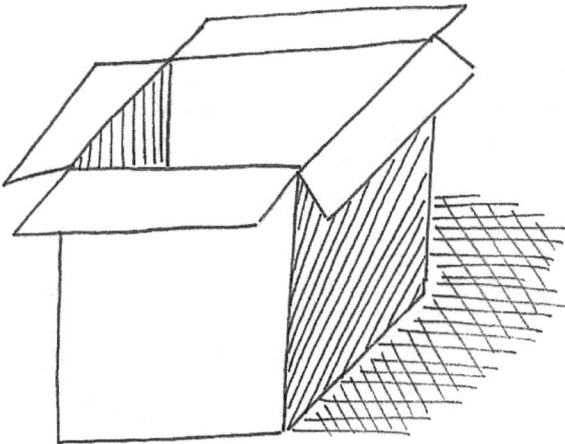

MY NAME IS...

My little peanut loves to ignore his given name
To this Mom it's exhausting, to him it's a fun game
"Tom! Dick! Harry! John!," I call out to him in vain
"Nope, you haven't guessed it!" He turns about to proclaim

"TOM!?"

"JOHN!?"

"JASON!?"

"JIMMY!?"

Trying to catch up to him as he darts around the mall
I call out, "Jason! Terrance! Oh, heck! Monty Hall!"
But the kid continues to ignore me, oh, the mounting gall
I cry, "Jimmy!" And he replies, "No! Today my name is, Paul."

I'M GONNA TURN BLUE

My little peanut loves to challenge my "No", with a pout
Sometimes holding his breath, until he almost blacks out
Hoping mommy will freak and do a complete turnabout
Knowing he has lost, his silence becomes an unwelcomed shout.

The time has come to bid you adieu and farewell
We hope you found our adventures funny and swell
Hug your little peanut, but not enough to crack his shell
Until then, be merry, thankful and well.

THE END

P.S. -

"Let me know if you find my missing shoe."

www.ingramcontent.com/pod-product-compliance
Lightning Source LLC
Chambersburg PA
CBHW071800020426
42331CB00008B/2336